MW00917669

How to Breed a Rabbit

The Ultimate Guide to Bunny and Rabbit Breeding, Baby Rabbits and Rabbit Care.

By Sarah Martin

ISBN-13:
978-1495486470

ISBN-10:
1495486478

All inquiries should be addressed to:

Everything Rabbit

PO Box 1127#A1104

Quartzsite, AZ 85346

USA

www.EverythingRabbit.com

This book is a product of the United State of America

The information and advice in this book if for educational purposes only. All matters regarding health and wellness should be supervised by a licensed veterinary specialist.

Table of Contents

By Sarah Martin

QUICK STOP HERE!

Please check out our companion website at

www.EverythingRabbit.com

For Your Free Downloads

Included with your book are plans for building a mini rabbit transport cage, monthly health checklist (do this before you buy a rabbit!) and a chores checklist.

You can also sign up for our newsletter, find answers to all your rabbit questions & connect with others in the bunny community.

Please visit us and help support our quest to deliver great rabbit information!

A portion of our proceeds go towards supporting free rabbit education and 4-H clubs.

Thank you for purchasing our book. If you enjoyed out book <u>please leave a review on Amazon</u> so that we can make our future revisions even better!

Introduction

One of the most rewarding and memorable moments of any rabbit breeder's life is when they have their first litter of baby bunnies. A lot of steps need to happen to ensure that those little balls of fur come into this world happy & healthy but that's why you bought this book, right?

Breeding rabbits is a great hobby and can actually generate a nice side income, more money to feed your rabbit habit. Congratulations on taking your first steps towards being a responsible baby bunny parent and learning the details and techniques of how to breed a rabbit.

A fuzzy baby bunny might be one of the cutest animals on the planet. After reading this book, you will soon be enjoying time with your very own litter of tiny rabbits!

Everyone always jokes about "breeding like rabbits" but a lot more goes into a successful mating than just the breeding and to be a responsible pet owner (and enjoy your time with your new bunny family), you need to know the ins and outs of the entire breeding, birthing, and raising experience.

This book is step-by-step guide to help lead you through the process of selecting your rabbits for breeding, how the mating ritual works, and what to expect while your rabbit is pregnant and after she gives birth (baby time!).

I'll also reveal details on how to care for your new babies, all the equipment/feeding info you'll need, and go into troubleshooting in case something goes wrong (this is stuff you need to know!).

If you are new to rabbit breeding, or just want to expand your depth of knowledge, then you will find everything you need and more in the following chapters.

This will be a fun & exciting time for new rabbit parents, so keep reading to find all the great information on how to breed your first batch of bunny babies.

Chapter 1

What Should I Know About Rabbit Breeding Before I Start?

Before you breed your first rabbit there are a few critical things to think about. In this chapter, we'll go over rabbit terms (that are commonly used by rabbit breeders), explore why you're breeding your rabbits and look into ways to match up a good breeding pair.

Making sure that you are matching up a good male/female rabbit pair is one of the most critical steps before mating and will also be a very important factor in ensuring your rabbit's pregnancy goes well.

Rabbit Breeding Basics

Before we dig into the world of breeding rabbits lets go over a few, quick terms that I'll be using throughout this book:

- o   Buck: a male rabbit.

- Doe: a female rabbit.

- Pair: the male & female rabbit that you breed together.

- Kit(s): baby rabbit(s).

- Kindle: when a rabbit gives birth.

- Litter: used to refer to the entire group of newly born kits.

- Foster: to take a newborn kit & place it in another doe's litter for her to raise.

- Herd: Your entire group of rabbits, including adults & babies (kind of like a herd of buffalo, only cuter & fluffier).

- Nest Box: the box that the mama rabbit builds her nest in.

- Vent: the doe sex organ.

- In Heat: the time immediately preceding ovulation, it is when the doe is most fertile and also the most receptive to mating.

- Conception: The act of baby rabbits being conceived through the union of the male sperm and the female ovum, fertilization = making babies.

- ○ Gestation Period: The time from conception to birth.

- ○ Palpate: A process of checking a doe's belly to see if she is pregnant, usually done on the 14th day after mating.

- ○ Wean: When the kits no longer need their mother's milk and are removed from her cage.

Before you start thinking about breeding your rabbits, you need to take a few things into consideration to make sure you match up a good breeding pair. One of the first things to consider is…

Are you breeding for pet, show or farm rabbits?

Pet Rabbits: Can be any combo of cute and adorable furry bunnies that you choose to breed together. The only note of caution I would add is to make sure that your rabbits are in good health & that they do not have any genetic conditions that you wouldn't want to pass on to the next bunny generation, such as bad teeth or blindness.

Pet rabbits can also be harder to sell after the litter is old enough to be taken away from their mother. There is a larger market for show rabbits (and showing rabbits is a TON of fun), so consider purchasing and breeding show-worthy rabbits (purebreds) if you truly want to start breeding rabbits year round.

There is an over population of pet rabbits in the world that don't have a home and end up in shelters all over the country. The world doesn't need more abandoned pet so act responsibly with any rabbit breeding project and be sure that you can find good homes for any bunnies you will not be keeping.

Show Rabbits: There is an alive & thriving show world for rabbits (just like showing dogs) and participating in rabbit shows can be a great way to enjoy your new bunny additions and also sell the babies that you don't want to keep.

To show a rabbit you will need to have pure breed stock that meets with the current "standards" that are in place for show rabbits.

You can find all sorts of information about show rabbits from the American Rabbit Breeders Association and on our website www.EverythingRabbit.com (you can also see examples of different breeds and read about their pros and cons).

I would recommend, for anyone interested in show rabbits, that they start investigating what breed of rabbit they want (there are over 100 breeds worldwide) and then find a rabbit breeder to purchase stock from. You can find a great article on locating breeders in your area on our site by going to www.EverythingRabbit.com and click on the "New to Rabbits?" tab. The American Rabbit Breeders Association also has great resources for locating breeders, you can visit their website at www.ARBA.net.

Farm Rabbits: From hobby farms to family homesteads, rabbits are gaining massive popularity as an easy-to-raise meat animal that can also double as a source of wool, fur, and fertilizer (rabbit manure is excellent for your garden).

Farm rabbits are usually chosen for their over-all meat quality and hardiness. If you're interested in raising farm rabbits then I would recommend starting with any of the breeds that are classified as "Commercial Type" (such as New Zealand's or Californians), these breeds are specifically developed for meat and fur production.

Is it a Boy or a Girl? Determining the Sex of Your Rabbit.

It's always helpful to be able to determine if your rabbit is a buck or doe before you attempt to breed.

To examine your bunny's private area, you should pick up your rabbit and gently hold them by the shoulder, then roll them over onto their back. Clip their tail between your #1 and #2 fingers and then use your thumb to move their fur & expose the genitals.

Male rabbits (bucks), past 6 months old, should have a penis and two testicles visible once you move all the fur. A female (doe) will just have a small vent area with an opening. (see photo for examples)

By Sarah Martin

Male Rabbit

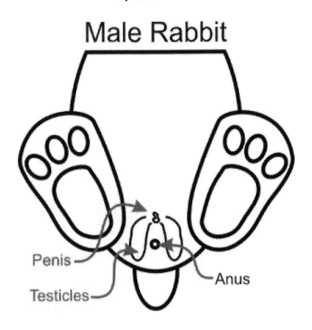

Penis

Testicles

Anus

Female Rabbit

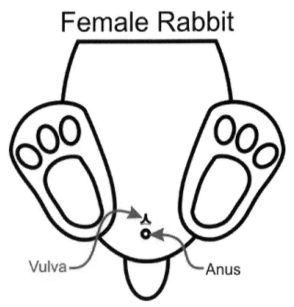

Vulva

Anus

Has your rabbit been spayed or neutered?

This may seem obvious, but you'll want to make sure that neither of your rabbits have been spayed or neutered, since that would eliminate any option of breeding those rabbits together.

Most of the time, if you've purchased your bunnies from a pet store or a breeder, this won't be a problem for you. If you have a rescue rabbit from a shelter check your adoption paperwork because the shelter may have already spayed or neutered your rabbit.

Matching up Your Rabbit Pair – looks and size matters.

Size:

The doe's (female rabbit) over-all body size will affect the outcome of the mating. Small does that are bred to large bucks can cause a birthing problem because the babies may be too large to pass through the doe's smaller birth canal.

Take this into account when matching up your rabbit pair and try to keep your buck and doe around the same size, within a pound or two of each other's weight.

Additionally, rabbit breeds that have large heads and narrow hips/small bodies (like Nederland Dwarfs and Holland Lops) are notorious for getting "stuck" babies, not a fun thing for your first rabbit litter. If you are a beginner breeder then try to choose a doe with nice, wide hips for your first mating to avoid this problem. If your doe has narrow hips she can have a harder time during delivery.

The size of your breeding pair will also play a big role in the number of babies in the litter.

Smaller rabbits will produce smaller litters. A little dwarf-type breed, that only weighs two or three pounds, will generally have two to four kits (baby rabbits) at a time. A larger sized rabbit, in the eight to ten pound range (or bigger), can easily have a litter of eight to twelve kits or more!

Make sure you are prepared for the potential size of the litter; you may need twelve extra cages just to house all your new babies if you are breeding large rabbits.

Looks:

Another thing to think about when you match up your pair is the over-all looks of the two rabbits. If you are breeding a show rabbit there is an entire art to combining different elements from different rabbits to get a beautiful show bunny.

I recommend buying a copy of the current Standard of Perfection from the American Rabbit Breeders Association to use as a guide when breeding show rabbits. This book is the Bible of show bunny perfection and is used by rabbit judges to determine if your rabbit is a good example of their breed.

If you are breeding for farming it's still a good idea to think about what the combo of the buck & doe will look like together. Like all offspring, the litter will have elements and traits from both parents (including personality!).

In-Breeding:

A word about in-breeding: In-breeding is when you breed related rabbits back to each other, like father to daughter or brother to sister. This is common practice in the world of show rabbits when a breeder is trying to selectively get a certain characteristic into their rabbit's offspring.

For beginning breeders, I would recommend staying away from this practice and, instead, start by breeding new genetic stock (a rabbit that is un-related to your existing rabbit). If you do decide to breed related animals then try to include new blood by at least every two generations.

Too much in-breeding can lead to some weird birth defects (I've seen pictures of rabbits born with half their ears gone or deformed legs), so use caution as you think about breeding genetically related bunnies.

Often times, I would recommend that you save in-breeding matings until after you have some experience in the whole rabbit breeding world and have a better idea of what to expect.

How You Can "Borrow" a Rabbit for Breeding

A great way to start out in rabbit breeding is to "go in" with another rabbit owner and breed a pair of rabbits together, with each of you will providing one rabbit. For example, if you have a doe and you're friend has a buck you can mate them together without ever needing to own the father-rabbit.

This can also be a great option for breeding show rabbits and a lot of rabbit breeders will just charge you a "stud fee" (a fee to breed your doe to one of their bucks) and you can start producing showable rabbit litters without having to buy two animals.

Another way to compensate the person who supplied the buck is to give them "pick of the litter" when the babies are born, which means that the male-rabbit owner takes a "fee" in the form of one of the baby rabbits (when they are old enough to be taken away from their mother). This way you have no money out the door, which is nice when you're first starting out.

I, myself, have "gone in" many times with other rabbit breeders & have found it a great way to do some interesting breeding combos without having to buy more rabbits to add to my herd. It's also a great way to build friendships with other rabbit breeders.

Think about breeding two does (female rabbits) on the same day.

One habit that I recommend, for beginners and advanced rabbit breeders alike, is to breed at least two does on the same day. This way you have a "backup" mama rabbit in case something goes wrong with one litter or with the other mama rabbit.

If you need to foster babies or something happens to one of the mama rabbits during delivery you will be very happy that you gave yourself this backup plan.

Rabbits are very accepting of new kits into their litters

(we'll talk about this in a later chapter) and hand raising a baby rabbit is hard to do and has a very low survival rate.

If you have more than one breeding doe in your herd then go ahead & mate at least two does on the same day.

If you're just starting out and only have one doe to breed you can still make sure you are covered, you just need to coordinate your mating so that it happens on the same day that someone else in your area is mating his or her rabbits. This is where it pays to have other friends who are breeding & raising rabbits.

If you don't know other breeders, don't fret! Start by searching for rabbit breeders in your area (Google or get in touch with the American Rabbit Breeders Association to find names), explain your situation to the breeder and ask if you can coordinate to mate your rabbit on the same day that they will be breeding some of their rabbits.

Most rabbit breeders are more than happy to help you and you could make a life-long friend with your new connection. They can also be a great resource when you have questions or need help with your bunnies.

What will you do with the Babies? Being a Responsible Pet Owner.

A lot of people love the idea of having baby bunnies (which is totally understandable, they are crazy-cute!), but remember that you will be expanding your bunny family with two to twelve extra rabbits (depending on the size of the litter).

Rabbit ownership should be taken seriously so make sure that you are ready and willing to ensure that these new rabbits have a chance for a good life & home.

If you are planning on keeping the kits it's good to double-check that you have enough room to house all these new rabbits. You'll want to keep the boys & girls separated when they hit sexual maturity or you could end up with way more bunnies than you ever bargained for.

Selling or giving away the babies you don't want to keep is always an option, but remember, you will still need to house them until they are old enough to be weaned (not nursing from their mother anymore) or until you can find new homes for the babies.

Craig's list ads, 4-H clubs, feed stores and word-of-mouth are all good ways to find a new home for extra baby rabbits. If you are breeding show rabbits then you also have the added option to sell to other breeders and potential breeders, which can often generate a nice side income.

Here are a few things to think about to make sure you are prepared for those extra rabbits:

- The Babies: Make sure you have a plan for responsibly finding new homes for the offspring. Remember that the pet market might not be in great demand in your area so be prepared to hold onto your new rabbits, if needed, until you can find them new homes.

- Budget: Are you ready to feed more mouths? Luckily, rabbit food is not expensive but new cages, feeders and more of your time will need to be invested for any rabbits you add to your herd.

- Knowledge: Be sure to read this entire book before you start breeding and seek out the advice of other breeders before you start mating your own rabbits. You should know what you're getting into & be prepared if anything goes wrong during pregnancy or birth.

To recap the items outlined in this chapter, here are some guidelines to use when choosing a pair of rabbits to mate:

- <u>Size:</u> Make sure that the buck & doe are within about 2 pounds of each other's weight or the buck is smaller than the doe to minimize birthing complications.

- <u>Health:</u> Make sure both rabbits are healthy & free from any genetic defects that shouldn't be passed onto another generation of bunnies.

- <u>Remember that you can always "go in" on a mating</u> with another breeder and be the owner of only one of the rabbits in the pair.

- <u>Breed two does on the same day</u> or coordinate with another breeder, so that you have a backup litter to foster babies to, as needed, or if something goes wrong.

Chapter 2

When Should I Breed My Rabbits?

In this chapter we'll get into the specifics of how a rabbit's age can affect pregnancy, how to get the timing just right for your first breeding day and talk about how weather can affect your breeding schedule.

Rabbit Age. You're how old?

You usually safe to start breeding rabbits when they are five to six months old, by then most breeds have reached sexual maturity.

Exceptions to this would be if you have a very large rabbit (over ten pounds), it could take up to eight months for them to reach sexual maturity. Wait until your does are close to their final adult size before breeding them to make sure that they are ready to birth a litter.

You don't want to breed your does if they are too

young or you could stunt their growth and cause a whole group of health complications. Bucks (male rabbits), on the other hand, mature much quicker and can often impregnate a doe as early as twelve weeks old but bucks will also reach their full sexual maturity around six months of age.

Your doe's age can also play a big role in her having an easy, natural birth.

As your mama-rabbit ages her body doesn't adapt as well to the changes that take place during pregnancy and that can put both her and her litter at risk.

I don't recommend breeding a doe that is over two years old who has never had a litter before. Most of the time their bodies just can't take it and they end up having difficult births.

If your doe has had a litter before she was two years old than you are fine to continue breeding her up to 5 years old (and longer if she's still in good health).

As far as the buck rabbit goes, age is not as big a factor for breeding, although after age 5 (depending on their over-all health) sperm count starts to go down & the chance of conception is greatly decreased.

How can I tell if My Doe is in Heat?

One of the biggest natural factors that will affect breeding success is if the doe is "in heat" at the time of mating.

A doe will be in heat immediately preceding ovulation; it is when the doe is most fertile and also the most receptive to mating. If your doe is in heat before she breeds with the buck you will have a much higher success of conception.

You can usually tell when she's "ready" just by her behavior. Often times, all you'll do is touch her back & she'll spread out her body & raise her tail (which is the action she does right before the buck mounts her during mating).

Another way to check if your doe is in heat is to flip her over onto her back & examine her vent area (sex organ). If the vent is a little red in color and slightly swollen she is most likely in heat. The normal appearance of the vent, when a doe is not in heat, is a soft pink color.

What Time of Year should I Breed My Rabbits?

You should definitely consider the time of year when deciding to breed your rabbits. A normal gestation period (the time from conception to birth) for a doe to kindle (giving birth) after mating is 31 days.

If you are thinking of breeding your doe and it is the middle of winter and the temperature is -10 degrees outside, you might want to wait for spring if your rabbits aren't housed in a climate controlled area.

Adult rabbits are amazingly hardy & adaptive creatures that can survive in all sorts of environments, either extreme hot or cold, but, if you can choose, pick a time of year that has a more comfortable temperature. **Kits are much more venerable to temperature extremes** and you could lose litters because of the weather if you don't take steps to keep their nest box at a regulated temperature.

A comfortable, stable temperature will create less stress on the doe during pregnancy and birth; it will also increase the chances of raising a full litter. You will often lose one or two kits to weather related exposure during extreme times of hot and cold. This is especially true if you house your rabbits outside.

If you do decide to breed during extreme weather take the following recommendations into account:

Hot Weather: Hot weather can take a bigger toll on your rabbit's health than cold. Rabbits don't sweat so to cool down they use their ears like a big radiator to dissipate heat, that's why wild rabbits that live in the desert have such big ears!

This also means that, if your rabbit has smaller or floppy lopped ears, they will have a much harder time getting rid of extra body heat (at least, much more so than their wild cousins, who have it made in the shade with their gigantic ears).

When the temperature outside starts to spike it can get really brutal for your rabbits if they are housed outside. When I first started breeding rabbits I lived in Arizona, during the summer it could get well over 110 degrees in the middle of the Sonoran Desert.

That kind of heat will put significant stress on your animals, so I always avoided breeding during the extreme summer months. But, if you need to, here are a few tips and tricks to help keep your rabbits cool.

- **Frozen two liter soda bottles** can become a rabbit-cooling machine: Fill empty soda bottles with water, freeze, and place them in your rabbit's cage so your bunny can snuggle up against them. Replace with new frozen bottles every morning.

- **Water misters:** Water misters are a great way to help keep your rabbits cooler during the summer, although, if the water is spraying directly on their fur it can cause some discoloration so make sure the rabbit has a way to get out of the water & never have water spraying directly onto your baby bunnies. Water misters are available at pool supply stores and in the garden section of most mega-super-stores.

- **Homemade Swamp Coolers:** An inexpensive water mister, water hose, a fan and a damp towel draped over a rabbit's cage and you have yourself a homemade swamp cooler. Place the fan so it blows through the towel and then into your rabbit's cage and use the mister to keep the towel wet. Note that this method does not work well in humid climates, too much water in the air means no evaporation and no cooling down.

- **Just bring your rabbit inside!** Simple & easy, you can just move them inside during bad weather & move them back outside when it's nice.

Cold Weather: Most adult rabbits do very well in cold weather & adapt well to cold climates, the only exceptions being baby rabbits and breeds that have rex fur (rex fur is really short fur that feels like velvet) as their coat is too short to offer good protection from extreme cold.

A well-built nest by your mama rabbit will help to keep her babies warm and roasty toasty, even down into negative degree weather. But if your mama doesn't do a great job of building a nest you are left with a litter of kits that could freeze to death (no fun).

Here are a few extra tips to keeping your new babies nice and warm:

- **The Nest Box:** We'll talk about nest boxes in the equipment chapter but my one recommendation for cold weather is to use a wood nest box. I usually recommend metal ones for easy cleaning but I think they pull too much heat away from the babies when it's really cold out. Wood insulates better, so use it during the chilly times of the year.

- **A Small Portable Heater:** You can create a little "rabbit tent" with an old sheet or blanket (nonflammable!) and a portable heater. Just make sure the heater is rated for indoor/outdoor use and that you follow the entire manufacturer's instructions for setting the heater up.

- **Nest Box Heating Pad:** There are a few companies that specialize in small animal equipment that sell small heating pads specifically developed to fit inside a nest box and help keep it warm. All you would need is an extension cord to plug into and you would have a nice, warm nest for the babies. You can see examples in the "Stuff We Recommend" section of our website at www.EverythingRabbit.com or you can search for this item on Amazon.com.

- Just like with extreme hot weather, **you can always bring your rabbit inside!** Simple & easy, you can just move them inside during bad weather & move them back outside when it's warmed up or the kits are old enough to survive. I would recommend moving your doe inside before she has kindled and then moving everyone back outside after the babies are five to six weeks old. Use your judgment here – if it's still too cold for anything to do well outside then keep everyone in a temperature regulated environment until it safe.

Chapter 3

What Equipment Do I Need?

The equipment for nesting and baby bunny care is very straightforward & inexpensive, you can even make some of it yourself if you're a "handy" kind of person. In this chapter we'll review a list of the essential items you'll need to have before your rabbit gives birth.

Nest Box

Every mama-bunny-to-be will need somewhere to build her nest. Rabbit nest boxes are usually made from wood or metal with high sides and a lower front lip so the mama rabbit has an easy time jumping out but the lip is high enough to keep baby rabbits in.

Many nest boxes also have a covered roof over the top, which is especially nice in cooler months for keeping heat in the nest (most mama rabbits also like to sit up there).

Most nest boxes will be built with either a solid floor or a mesh floor that allows liquids to pass through the bottom.

My favorite kinds of nest boxes have all metal sides/roofs with a mesh floor. The mesh floor helps keep the interior of the nest box nice & dry and the metal is easy to clean when the babies are grown and you're ready for another litter.

Also note that rabbits like to chew on wooden nest boxes, so you also get the added bonus of metal lasting longer if you choose this style.

The only time I prefer using wooden nest boxes is during the cold winter months because the wood insulates much better than a metal nest box.

Another perk of the wooden nest boxes is that, with a saw, nails and some wood glue, you can make them yourself.

Metal nest boxes will need to be purchased from either a local feed store or online. You can view some different styles of nest boxes at our website in the Breeding Equipment section by going to www.EverythingRabbit.com and click on the "Stuff We Recommend" tab or you can search for this item on Amazon.com.

Nest Box Size:

The size of your nest box will depend on the size of your doe. She should be able to jump in and fit her entire body into the box and be able to barely turn around but have no more room than that.

The small space helps keep the kits confined in the box so they don't wander out of the nest area, which can lead to overexposure and death. The smaller size also means that your doe will be less likely to "hang out" in the box, which will keep the nest area cleaner.

Nest boxes come in all shapes & sizes, so finding a box to fit your bunny shouldn't be difficult. Don't forget to take the materials (wood or metal) into account when purchasing your nest box and choose the best style for your area and specific situation.

Nesting Material

Hay there! Hay is the material your rabbit will use to build her nest. Not just any old hay will do though; your doe will prefer soft, grassy hays like Timothy hay or Bermuda grass.

Don't give her alfalfa hay and other hays that have a stiff stalk. This variety of hay is too hard to bend and will make it difficult for you rabbit to dig out and form her nest.

Most pet stores and feed stores will have many different types of hay available and, as long as it passes the "bend" test, it should be fine for your rabbit's nest (see more on this below). You can see examples of various bags of good nesting-material hays in the Breeding Equipment section of our site, go to www.EverythingRabbit.com and click on the "Stuff We Recommend" tab or you can search for this item on Amazon.com.

The "bend" test is when you take a handful of the hay and try to bend the stalks into a circle. If the hay flexes and bends easily then it's going to work great for nesting material. If the stalks break and don't want to bend then move on to a different kind of hay. As mentioned, a few of my favorite hays are Timothy or Bermuda, which you can find in small to medium sized bags at any pet store mega-mart and at most local feed stores.

Once you've purchased your hay you're going to want to stuff your nest box. You'll need enough hay to fill your nest box approximately two-thirds of the way full and have a little extra left over to fill in whatever the mother-to-be decided to eat.

Keep extra hay on hand to replace eaten hay or any hay that become wet or soiled.

BONUS TIP:

Rabbits LOVE munching on Timothy & Bermuda hay so it can also double as a sweet treat for your furry friends, buy extra!

Breeding Calendar

Having a calendar dedicated to your breeding rabbits is a great way to keep track of litters, due dates and other important information.

I like to keep mine posted in an easy to see place, so that I **never forget when to put in the nest box or check for new kits.** It is also a nice reference for later, when you're breeding that same doe again, to check info about her last litter, when she delivered, the size of her litter and other rabbit breeding information.

I've heard stories of a rabbit breeder who lost track of the days and forgot to put in a nest box, their doe ended up delivering right on the cage floor. She ended up losing the entire litter just because she didn't keep a calendar. Don't let this happen to you, **stay on top of your breeding schedule!**

Be sure that you keep an accurate calendar with important due date listed. Stuff like adding the nest box to your doe's cage and expected delivery dates are very important to keep track of.

We'll cover all of these, in detail, in the next chapters.

Chapter 4

How do I Actually Mate My Rabbits?

Now… on to the action! In this chapter we will go over the entire mating processing including troubleshooting (if your rabbits don't want to mate) and other great tips and tricks for successful rabbit breeding. Time to dig into the details and start making baby bunnies!

How to - The 1st Mating

Now comes the fun part, time to let the rabbits get down to the business of baby making! So, you've checked that your doe is in heat (see previous chapter for how to check this) and you have romantic music playing in the background.

First thing you want to do is take the doe out of her cage, so she can meet up with the buck and they can get busy. You can let the doe & buck get together in one of two ways:

1. **Take the doe and place her in the buck's cage.** This is the most common method used by rabbit breeders.

Never take the buck and place him in the doe's cage; this can lead to some serious fighting! A female rabbit tends to be very territorial about her space and will often attack any other animal placed in her cage. Or...

---

2. **Have the two rabbit meet on "neutral territory."** Take out the buck first and place him on a flat surface with traction so he won't slip around, such as a carpet covered table or floor, and then take out the doe and set her next to the buck.

You would most commonly use this method when the one of the rabbit's is giving you trouble and wants to fight/ doesn't want to breed. It's much easier to control the situation when both rabbit's aren't defending "their space" and you can get to them quickly.

Either one of these options will keep the doe in neutral territory, so she will be less inclined towards violence and she will be more inclined to go along with the mating.

Your doe can get rather grumpy when she's in heat, so always make sure you are watching her and the buck when they are together so nothing turns ugly. It doesn't happen very often but I've heard of angry does biting off things that, I'm sure the buck would have preferred to keep intact.

Once your rabbits are together the whole mating process will happen very quickly. They might sniff each other for a minute or two and then the buck will start to mount the doe.

If your doe is in heat she should respond by flipping up her tail and stretching out her body to make it easier for the buck to do his thing.

The buck will sometimes grab a chunk of fur, in his mouth, off the doe's back when he mounts her. Don't worry about this, its normal mating behavior.

Right after the mating has been completed (touchdown!) the buck usually flops over to the side and/or starts grunting very loudly. Don't worry he's not dead! Once again, this is normal behavior.

Once that has happened mating is complete and you can return everyone to their original cages. We will breed them again in another hour or two (see "The 2nd Mating" below).

Ideally all your breeding endeavors would be this simple but some rabbits will need a little help before they mate. If things don't seem to be going the way you want here are a few troubleshooting tips to help your rabbits complete the mating process.

If the doe starts mounting the buck, don't be too concerned here, it seems to be normal behavior for almost a 1/3 of breeding does. They just get excited and start going at it on their own.

If it continues for more than a few seconds or you see the buck starting to get frustrated then pull her off and gently hold her head so she can't keep mounting the buck and so he has time to get up there and do his thing.

The buck mounts the doe's head instead of her behind. This happens when the buck gets too excited and starts mounting any body part of the doe that he can. Often all you'll need to do is gently drag him around to the correct end and then nature will take it from there.

The doe attacks the buck when he tries to mount her. Like we said earlier, does can get cranky when they're in heat and sometimes need a little time to calm down before mating.

If the buck is overly enthusiastic she can get annoyed and go after him. Often times all you need to do is hold her head still (to make sure she can't turn and bite a chunk out of the buck) and he'll be able to mount her and the mating will be complete.

Other times it's just not going to happen and you'll need to try again at a later time for the safety of both the animals. If your doe isn't in full heat yet (or in a bad mood) she will sometimes resist mating. Wait a day and try again.

The buck has no interest in the doe. Less common, but it does happen. You put the rabbits together and they just stare at each other like an awkward first date. The buck seems to have no interest in mating and just gives her a sniff and wanders away.

Here is when you'll have to "explain" your expectation to him. Take the doe and wave her vent area in front of his face, if she's in heat he will be able to smell that (which is often enough to get his engine running).

Also try placing her on a table with her body stretched out and her tail up, and then place the buck on top of her as if he had mounted her. This often is enough for the buck to get the hint & start mating.

If none of this seems to be working, be patient. I once had a buck that seemed to suffer from stage fright and it took him 5-10 minutes before he could get his business on with the ladies.

If all else fails then wait a day and try again. Sometimes, if the doe is not in full heat the buck can have little or no interest in trying to mate with her.

If you've waiting a few days and still haven't gotten your rabbits to mate, it's time to think about breeding a different rabbit, either a buck or doe, depending on who is being the problem-maker.

This is where it's nice to have other friends who own rabbits so you can "go in" on a litter with another breeder, as mentioned in the previous chapter.

How to - The 2ⁿᵈ Mating

It is common practice to do a second mating of the same rabbit pair, on the same day that they've completed their 1st mating.

Plan on getting them back together within one to two hours of the 1st mating. You can go up to twelve hours between mating times, if needed, but it seems like they really stay "in the mood" within those first couple of hours.

After the 1st mating the doe will have released her eggs, so taking her to the buck a second time will help increase the chances of conception and pregnancy.

Rabbit Breeders Legend – Full Moon:

There is a legend going around the rabbit-breeding world for years now that, if you breed your rabbits during a full moon, you will drastically increase their chances of getting pregnant. No one is entirely certain where this idea came from but, if you're feeling like a night owl, give it a try!

I know one rabbit breeder who has been experimenting with this technique and she swears that it has increased the over-all success rate of pregnancy and that her rabbits have larger litters when bred on a night with a full moon.

If you experiment with this & it works let me know (you can email me at Sarah@EverythingRabbit.com) – there could be a whole new factor in mating that the rabbit world needs to know about!

By Sarah Martin

Chapter 5

Now What? After Mating and Waiting for Babies.

Now that you've mated your first pair of rabbits is time to get ready for babies! In this chapter we'll look at a typical pregnancy time lines and go over everything you'll need to do to get ready for your first litter, including checking to see if the doe is pregnant and when you need to give her a nest box.

To start, grab your breeding calendar. After mating your pair of rabbits it's time for some paperwork! Open up your calendar (or iPad) and mark down the day that you bred your pair.

Now we're going to also write in some important dates for your soon-to-be-mama bunny.

We'll get into more details on these as this chapter progresses but, for now, mark these days in your breeding calendar. Start with the day you mated your rabbits and counting out from there:

Day 14: Palpate – We will check to see if the doe is pregnant. (More details below.)

Day 21: Free Feed - Time to give the doe all the food she can eat.

Day 28: Nesting Begins - Put the nest box (with hay) into the doe's cage.

Day 28-34: Kindling – We're expecting birth and babies!

The average gestation (time between mating and when your doe gives birth) is 31 days. That means that on day 31 you will have baby bunnies if the pregnancy "took".

Rabbits are amazingly consistent in their birthing schedule and most does will give birth within one day of that "average 31 day" gestation period but they can kindle (a rabbit term for "giving birth") as early as 28 days or as late as 34.

How can I tell if she pregnant?

Day 14: Palpate the doe.

On day 14 we are going to "palpate" which

means checking your doe's belly to see if you can feel any babies inside.

You can try as early as 10 days but I find that waiting those extra 4 days makes it much easier to find the kits inside her abdomen.

Your rabbit will never get "really fat" or have any other super-obvious outward clues that she is carrying babies, so this is one of the few ways of checking to see if she is pregnant.

To Palpate: Start by taking your rabbit out of her cage. Sit on a comfy chair or couch & place her in your lap with her head pointing towards your stomach.

We're going to "feel around" in her abdomen to see if we can find any grape-sized balls in there (those would be the babies!). Use caution though – mama rabbits can get cranky as they advance along in their pregnancy. Be very gentle with this and use light pressure, you don't want to damage the forming kits.

To start, put your hand under her belly and, using your thumb and middle finger, start feeling around her tummy slowly working your way up towards the area where her back legs meet her belly. Use small circular motions when doing this, the same motion you would use to massage your temples if you had a headache.

Keep moving up her belly towards the back legs, while gently pushing upwards and inwards towards her vent area and the spot where her thighs meet her body. You'll end up with her back legs straddling your hand while you feel around.

The babies will feel like a small series of grapes or marbles all strung together with a thread. They should be soft and you should be able to feel them on either side of her belly. If you feel hard little balls those are not babies and are probably just poo pellets that haven't been expelled yet.

Be patient with this process, it takes practice and you might not get it right the first time. It could take a few litters before you get a feel for the technique.

Keep practicing and don't worry if you don't feel anything that could be babies, your doe might still be pregnant!

Some does have the tendency to "suck up air" when they are tense or being held and that can pull the forming babies further up into their abdomen, making it harder to tell if she is or isn't pregnant.

Should I Feed My Pregnant Rabbit Extra Food?

Day 21: All the food a rabbit could eat.

If you've determined (or suspect) that your doe is pregnant it's now time to up her quantity of food.

You should fill up her food bowl and let her eat as much as she wants during her last week of pregnancy. This will give your doe the extra calories and nutrients she needs for her growing babies.

If it turns out that your rabbit is not pregnant don't worry about the extra food. She can lose any extra weight in a few weeks after returning to a normal feeding schedule.

When Should I Give Her a Nest Box?

Day 28: Put the Nest Box into the cage.

In between day 21 and 28 you may have noticed some strange behavior from your doe. She may seem agitated and moving around a lot in her cage. Some does will also start scratching and pawing at the corner of their cages.

If your rabbit has a cage that allows them to sit in shavings (or some other type of bedding material) you may even notice her digging out a small hole and starting to line it with fur from her belly.

These are all signs of a rabbit that is ready to start nesting.

On day 28 take a nest box that's been stuffed with soft hay (refer back to our equipment section if you need a refresher on this) and place the box in your doe's cage.

All rabbits like to pick a corner of their cage to "do their business" and we want to avoid putting the nest box in the poo corner so pick a side of the cage that is easy for you to get to (you're going to want to be able to handle and check on these babies) and that is out of the rabbit-potty zone.

I usually place the nest box directly in front of the cage door & then push it back so that the back of the nest box is against the back cage wall. This makes it easy for me to get in and out without having to reach inside the entire cage.

Some mama rabbits will feel the need to move this box around the cage so don't be too surprised if you come in the next day & it's not exactly where you left it. You can always move it back or let the pregnant bunny have her way and leave it where she puts it.

If you notice that the doe starts using the nest box as a litter box instead, and starts pooping inside the box, go ahead and clean out the hay/nest box, put in fresh hay and move it to another corner of her cage.

She's Nesting! Now What?

With the nest box in your doe's cage she should start building her nest inside, if she is pregnant. This is one of the most fun times in the breeding/kindling process to watch.

Soon your doe will start taking mouthfuls of hay and move them around this way & that way. **She'll bite the hay off to just the right size and start building a circular nest (kind of like a birds nest) inside her nest box.**

Most does seem to really love this process and they are very busy getting it just right. She'll spend all day (and then some) working on this rabbit masterpiece for her new babies to call home.

Once she's placed all the hay exactly where she wants it, she will start plucking fur from her belly to line the nest. Her fur makes a nice, soft layer for the babies to sit on and it keeps the kits warm and insulated against cool weather.

Don't be surprised if you come out the next morning & see a nest box FULL of fur, some does go overboard with this and it looks like there is a whole other rabbit inside that box!

Also note that some does will pluck fur WAY in advanced of the litter and then others will wait until right before they give birth to do this. Don't be concerned if you don't see a lot of fur in the nest box before kindling, your rabbit may just be waiting for babies before she pulls fur.

If it doesn't look like your doe is interested in building a nest don't fret, sometimes that maternal nest-building instinct takes a little more time to kick in.

I always **leave the nest box in the cage until the 35th day after mating**, just to make sure she has somewhere to kindle if she is pregnant.

If it's been 35 days and your doe hasn't given birth then you can remove the nest box, wait for her to come into heat and then breed her again.

Some does will also go through a "false pregnancy" and will build a nest even though they aren't pregnant. If this happens to you feel free to leave the nest box in her cage an extra day or two just to be sure she isn't pregnant. If she still hasn't kindled after that then you are fine to breed her and try again.

Nest Box Troubleshooting: When a doe tries to build a nest in her cage outside the nest box.

Every now and then a doe will decide that the spot you placed the nest box in is not the "right" spot and she will proceed to remove all the hay from the box and move it to a corner of her cage that is the right spot...

Don't panic, just carefully pick up her nest material and place it back in the next box. Now move the nest box into the spot that she picked to build her nest.

This is usually enough of a hint for the doe to realize she is supposed to build her nest INSIDE the box but you will sometimes have to repeat this process two or three times with really stubborn does. Keep at it until she decides that you're right and the nest box is the best place for her to have her babies.

What Should I Do When She Gives Birth? Kindling

Day 28-34:

Your doe will probably deliver her litter in the

middle of the night when you're not around (tricky rabbits seem to plan it that way!), so don't worry about constantly watching her cage. Check on your doe a few times a day, I suggest morning and evening, when you're waiting for babies.

After she has delivered:

You will walk out one day & the inside of the fur-covered nest box will look likes it's moving a little bit (if you watch the fur really closely you can see it wiggling).

Congratulations! You are now a proud bunny parent!

You may also notice that there is quite a bit more fur inside the nest box after your doe has kindled. Many rabbits will pull extra fur after giving birth to cover over the babies.

If the nest box isn't full of fur and the babies look like they are not fully covered you may need to pluck some extra belly fur from the mother rabbit, especially if it's even a little chilly where they are housed.

A rabbit's fur-covered nest is one of the BEST WAYS to keep the babies warm and protected; an under-furred nest can lead to exposure and death for the kits.

The babies should have a layer of fur covering over the top of them, it doesn't need to be very thick but it should be there.

You can take the mama-rabbit and pluck extra fur, if needed, to cover the nest. The fur on her belly will be very loose after giving birth and should come off easily. Sometimes just the act of pulling a little fur will trigger a reaction in her and she'll keep plucking to cover her nest after you've placed her back in her cage.

This process also helps to expose the nipples for the kits to suckle.

Most mama-rabbits will pull enough fur on their own and won't require any help. But every now and then you'll have a doe that needs to be helped out with this, especially if they are a new mother.

Handling the Babies – Don't be Concerned about Spreading Your Scent to the Babies:

For domesticated rabbits it's a myth that you can't touch the babies because, if you do, the mother won't take care of them.

Your mother rabbit is very use to your scent & you being around. Plus, it's important to inspect the kits once they are born and to handle them often so they become accustom to people.

How do I Handle Newborn Kits (Baby Rabbits)?

Newborn kits should be handled gently but firmly.

Before you start handling the babies we need to see how your doe reacts to you coming close to her nest. Before trying to pick up a kit first open your doe's cage and place your hand inside the nest box. Wait a moment before you try to pick up any of the kits. We're taking stalk of the doe's reaction to you being in her nest.

Some does will be very protective of their new litter and you may have to remove the nest box from her cage to inspect the babies because she won't want to let you near them. If your doe is acting protective and grunts/ seems aggressive towards you don't worry, most mothers will calm down after a few days.

If needed, you may want to remove the whole nest box from the cage to inspect the babies and then return the box to the cage after you're finished. This way an aggressive doe will not be able to harm you and won't become agitated by your movements. The mother rabbit will usually calm down once the nest is removed and out of her line of sight.

If the mother rabbit doesn't seem to mind that you are in her nest box then don't worry about removing it from the cage to inspect the babies, as long as you can reach comfortably inside you can leave the nest box where it is.

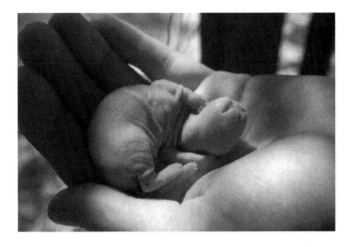

Now that you are in front of the nest box, pull back the fur pile that the mother made, to expose the newborn baby rabbits.

Go through our 5-point inspection outlined below and be sure to pick up every kit in the nest and make sure they look healthy and well fed.

Handling Caution:

Watch out when picking up kits! Baby rabbits can move so fast that they seem to pop like popcorn and you want to make sure you don't drop anyone! Cradle them in your hand so that, even if they start squirming, you won't lose them.

Here's a 5-point inspection of what you need to do when you have a newborn litter:

1. Move the fur off the kits (don't forget to put this back when you're done) and check to make sure they are all alive. It is common to have still born kits that are dead at birth and these should be removed from the nest box immediately.

   It's also common to have a runt of the litter (a baby with a super-small body size), so if you see a baby that is a lot smaller than the others, you have a runt. I usually leave them in the nest & root for them! Not many runts will survive past their first week (but some do!).

   > These runt babies, if they do mature to adulthood, will always be smaller than their littermates.

2. Check and see if there is any leftover placenta inside the cage or nest box. **Most does will eat the placenta right after delivery because it gives them a boost of nutrients and triggers hormonal changes in the doe.** But if there is

still any in the cage or nest box she's not going to touch what's left. Remove it and dispose, clean any areas that need cleaning.

3. **Check for the number of kits.**
   If your rabbit has delivered only one kit, it can be very hard for that kit to survive because it can't stay warm on its own. Baby rabbits huddle together for warmth.

   This is when you'll be very happy to have another doe with a litter available (if you took our advice and bred at least two does) and I would recommend fostering that baby into another litter to increase its chances of survival. See "Fostering Kits" below for details.

   If your rabbit has delivered more than ten kits, which can be very common in the larger breeds, you will probably want to foster some of those babies to a smaller litter so that there is enough milk for everyone.

   Ideally you'd like to have litter sizes of no more than eight kits at a time but some does are able to handle larger litters (and some... not so much). Keep an eye on large litters and act accordingly if the babies start to look like they're not getting enough food.

4. **Check for rounded tummies on the kits.** This means that mom is feeding them and everything is fine in the world of nursing.

   If you ever find that a kit (or kits) start to look thin & emaciated, you will want to think about fostering that kit(s) out to another mama rabbit because there may be a problem with their mother's milk supply or she may have too many kits in the litter and can't feed them all.

   We will also cover bottle feeding future in this chapter, but I would only recommend that as a last resort. It is much easier to foster kits to another litter, if needed, and the survival rate is much higher than if you try to bottle feed.

5. **Check that the doe has pulled enough fur to keep her babies warm**, especially if its winter. The nest should have enough fur to cover over the babies. If you need to, you can encourage your doe to pluck a little more fur by gently tugging at her belly fur (it loosens up right

around the time they give birth) and placing it in the nest.

Continue to check over the babies, one by one, until you have looked at every kit in the nest box.

Once you're done with your inspection place everyone back in their cozy nest, make sure to cover those babies back up with the fur pile you moved at the beginning of this process, and place the nest box back where it was in the doe's cage.

It's a good practice to look over all your babies at least once a day and make sure that everything is going well for both mother and kits.

Mother rabbits only feed their kits once or twice a day (yeah – that's it!) so don't be concerned if you don't ever see her in the nest box. As long as all the kits have fat bellies everyone is happy and the mother is doing her job.

Chapter 6

What Should I Do if Something Goes Wrong? Troubleshooting Common Birthing Problems

Ideally your first litter would happen exactly as described above but, unfortunately, things don't always go as planned.

In this chapter we'll review a breakdown of common birthing problems that may come up and what you can do about them.

First Time Mama Rabbits

When a doe has her very first litter she will be figuring out how this whole "having babies" thing works and she may not be a great mom on her first go around. Be patient with her, she will most likely improve with having more litters.

It is common to find that first-time does have their

babies on the cage floor instead of in the nest box. If this happens to you, and you get to the babies before they die from exposure, place them in the nest box and cover them with fur from the mama rabbit's belly (plucking a little more from her if you need to).

If the entire litter dies before you can get to them, chalk it up to your doe's inexperience and try breeding her again. I've had some does that took a few times to get it right and then ended up being great mothers for years to come.

Another thing you may experience (especially with first time mothers) is the doe chewing at or eating her kits.

While not pretty, this can happen and you could end up losing the entire litter or the kits could be missing an ear or a foot. Sometimes this behavior can be caused by the rabbit being panicked or frightened; perhaps by a loud noise or some large animal nearby, and other times there is no explanation.

I use a "three strike and you're out" approach to does that have kindling problems and if a doe continues with this behavior for three litters then she should be put into "retirement" and not bred anymore. It's just not worth loosing litters to a rabbit that might not be cut out to take care of kits.

Stillborn Kit

As mentioned earlier, it is very common for a litter to have a stillborn kit or two, especially if the litter size is very large.

This is just part of how nature works and, when you start breeding rabbits, you will realize that every kit isn't going to make it. Instead of focusing on the stillborn kits, focus on the kits that made it and the great adventure of becoming a rabbit parent and breeder.

All stillborn or dead kits should be removed from the nest box upon discovery.

Stillborn or Lost Litter

Sometimes a doe is just not having any luck and her entire litter can be stillborn. While rather uncommon, if this does happen to your doe, wait a week or so and breed her again.

Something may have gone wrong during her pregnancy or during birth that caused the litter to be stillborn, so give her another chance. If she continues to deliver stillborn litters then it's time to retire her from breeding and find another doe.

Stuck Babies or Difficulty Giving Birth

One of the most unfortunate things that can happen to a doe while she is giving birth is for her babies to become stuck in the birth canal & she can't deliver them on her own.

This is most common with rabbit breeds that have small bodies but BIG heads (like Netherland Dwarf or Holland Lops). Is can also be common when a doe was bred to a much larger buck or when the doe has really narrow hips which can make it hard to pass her kits through the birth canal.

This can also happen when a doe is getting older (past two years old) and has never been bred before. You can refer back to our section above on "When Should I Breed My Rabbits – Age" for more details on this.

Some does will handle a stuck baby on their own by pulling the kits out of the birth canal, which usually results in a loss of the litter (and it's not pretty to see) but the mother usually recovers and is fine after a few days.

If you see that your doe has been struggling to give birth, pushing and pushing but nothing is happening, then it is likely that she has stuck babies. This is when it's time to pull out the big guns and help her deliver her kits if you want to make sure that she survives the pregnancy.

If you have a vet or are friends with an experienced rabbit breeder this would be a good time to call them. A vet will be able to help things along with the mother and is always a good first choice.

If a vet is not an option for you there are a few things you can do to help her along.

> **NOTE: These are for emergency circumstances only and should only be used when you are certain that your doe is really struggling to give birth.** When in doubt it's always safe to consult with a veterinarian and/ or an experienced rabbit breeder.

To Help A Doe Deliver Stuck Babies:

You'll want to remove the rabbit from her cage and set her on a flat surface. The floor with a towel under her is always a good place to start.

Often she will get so exhausted from pushing (and nothing happening) that she'll start to run out of energy and will need some help delivering any kits still in her womb. If you see a baby start to immerge from the birth canal you can gently pull on it, in time with her contraction and when she pushes, to help her deliver. Continue this process until she has finished delivering her kits.

The kits will usually not survive this procedure but, if any do, place them in the nest and keep an eye on them and on the mother to make sure that everyone is OK. If a day or two passes and she is nursing the kits (evident by their fat bellies) then you're in the clear.

Fostering Kits to another Litter

Fostering kits is a very straightforward process and most does seem more than willing to accept new babies into their litters. Always **try to make sure that the litters are within a few days of the same age** when swapping babies from one nest box to another, it will make the transition easier for both mother and kit.

Mother rabbits also produce a special kind of milk, called colostrum, immediately after the birth of her litter. This first milk is nutrient-packed and an important part of a babies diet. Making sure that the litters you foster a baby to are within the same age will also keep the young on the same milk-schedule.

To Foster a Kit Into another Litter:

First, distract the doe that will be taking on these new

kits by placing a treat or something in her cage to keep her busy.

Take the kit(s) that needs to be fostered and bring them to their new nest box home. Pull back the fur covering the existing litter and place the new kits inside.

Rub the new kits with the fur inside the nest and make sure all the babies are in a nice group around each other.

These new kits will take on the smell of the fur and the smell of the existing kits, so the doe will start feeding them and treating them like her own. Mama rabbits are very accepting of new additions to their litter and will usually continue on as if nothing has happened.

Bottle-Feeding Kits (How to Hand Raise Baby Rabbits)

A Harsh Fact: Bottle-feeding a newborn rabbit is not easy and the survival rate for the kits is usually less than twenty percent.

If your kits are older than two weeks you'll have a higher success rate than that, but it is very low with newborns. **I always recommend fostering as a first choice** if at all possible but, if necessary, you can bottle-feed and hand raise kits.

If you happen to know someone who has milking goats this can be a great rabbit milk substitute. You'll want the raw goat milk for your kits, not store bought pasteurized milk. I've know several rabbit breeders who were able to successfully raise kits off of their neighbor's goats milk.

If that's not an option for you then see below for a rabbit milk replacement recipe.

Bottle-Feeding Milk Recipe:

You'll have to make a trip to the pet store/grocery store to pick up a few supplies, here's what you'll need:

- Very small bottle (kitten sized) or syringe for the milk.
- Nipples for the bottle.
- Kitten Milk Replacer (usually sold by the can at any pet store mega-mart)
- Heavy Cream
- Goats Milk, fresh is best so if you can find it, get it!
- OPTIONAL - FOR NEWBORN RABBITS UP TO TWO WEEKS OLD: Freeze-dried lyophilized colostrum (which you can usually find at high-end health food stores or from your

veterinarian). This ingredient is not necessary but a mother rabbit produces colostrum in her milk right after the birth of her litter so it will give the kits a better chance of survival if they are very young.

To make the formula: Mix a 1/3 of a cup of the Kitten Milk Replacer with a 1/3 a cup of the goat's milk, add a teaspoon of heavy cream (and one tablespoon of colostrum, if you purchased it).

Store all extra formula in the fridge inside a sealed container and mix new formula every 2 days (or when you run out). Only add colostrum for the first two weeks of the kit's life and then make a formula mix without it.

To feed the kits, place the formula in a sterile container and heat to 105 degrees Fahrenheit (I use the microwave on a very low setting but you could also do this on the stovetop) and then put the milk mixture into the bottle or syringe.

Take a kit into your hand and place the bottle's nipple against the kit's lips. Some kits will automatically start sucking away but others will need to be convinced to eat.

Squeeze out a small drop of formula and place it on

the outside of the kit's lips. Now wait & be patient for the kit to lick it off.

Repeat this process until the kit is sucking from the bottle. **Note that it can take days for kits to accept bottle-feeding but you can get them through with the wetted lips and having them lick it off.** Continue feeding until you see their bellies become rounded.

Whatever you do when feeding newborn kits realize that the name of the game is patience! This process takes a lot of time for both the rabbit and the person trying to feed them but one of the worst things you could do is rush this and end up force-feeding the kit.

Never force the kit to take in formula. Rabbits have no way of throwing up so that excess liquid ends up going into their respiratory system and the kits usually die from an infection or suffocating.

Feeding Schedule: Feed your kits twice a day until they are old enough to start eating solid food, which will happen when they are around three to six weeks old.

Once they are old enough to eat solid food and are consuming it on their own you can move the feedings down to just once a day. You may even be able to give the kits a shallow bowl of formula and let them lick it up for themselves once they've reached this age.

Rabbits are usually weaned off of milk at 6 to 8 weeks of age, so start lessening the amount of milk you give them, starting at week 6, until they are off it completely by the end of week 8.

Other Things To Do When Hand-Raising Kits:

One other very important element to hand raising babies is stimulating them until they go to the bathroom. During the first two weeks of a kit's life they cannot pee or poop on their own – that's where you come in!

After feeding take a cotton ball or q-tip that has been barely moistened in warm water and start making small swipes around the kit's belly and genitals. Think of a mama rabbit licking her babies and you'll get an idea of the type of motion I'm talking about, it should be very light pressure.

Keep at it until you see that the kit has relieved themselves; you may want to have a paper towel handy to sop up any liquid.

Stimulating the kits to urinate and excrete is an important step to successfully raising kits by hand. You cannot skip it or the kits will die from a ruptured bladder/urinary tract.

If you decide to attempt to raise newborn kits by hand then remember to have patience and work slowly and gently. It can be a very trying experience but also a very rewarding one if you can successfully save your baby bunnies and raise them to be adults!

By Sarah Martin

Chapter 7

How do I Take Care of the Babies after Their Birth?

After your doe has kindled and you've checked that the litter is alive & being taken care of it's time to move onto the really fun part – the babies! In this chapter we'll talk about baby rabbit care & feeding along with a breakdown of what you'll need to do next in the bunny raising process.

Your new kits will be born with eyes closed and they will have almost hairless bodies. **For the first few weeks of their lives you shouldn't need to do anything for these babies, except check them over once a day and keep their mama fed and happy.**

Continue to give your doe as much food as she wants, you'll work it back down to her pre-baby food levels after the kits have been weaned (weaned meaning the kits have stopped drinking milk and can be removed from their mother's cage).

During this time it's very important to make sure the nest box stays clean and dry for the first few week of a kit's life or it can lead to infection. If an area inside the nest box becomes damp or dirty just scoop out the hay in that area and put in new hay.

One of the reasons that I love nest boxes with mesh bottoms is because moisture is seldom ever an issue, it just leaks out the through the mesh!

The kits should start opening their eyes when they are around ten to twelve days old. If you notice that gunk or a sticky residue is building up around their eyes you should clean it off with a warm, damp cotton ball or towel.

When the Babies Open Their Eyes

All your kits will open their eyes at different times so don't worry if some are open and some aren't. If any kits go past twelve days old and still have not opened their eyes, I will usually open them by hand. Just hold the kit and gently pull their eyelids apart until you can just start to see their eyes.

Kits Leaving the Nest Box before 12 Days Old

If any of the kits find their way out of the nest box during their first two weeks pick them up and place them back inside. Sometimes kits can get pulled out of the nest box if they are still holding onto the doe's teat when she jumps out but you don't want them to become sick or injured, just pick them up and tuck them back into their nest.

Leaving the Nest Box

The kits shouldn't start wandering out of the nest box until they are about twelve to eighteen days old, then they will start happily exploring their new world on wobbly little legs.

By day eighteen everyone should be out and jumping around, if you have a few stubborn kits still in the nest box then kick them out into the cage to join everyone else.

Removing the Nest Box

On day 18 you will remove the nest box entirely from the cage to help prevent infection and illness. Those boxes can become a breeding ground for bacteria after having so many rabbits inside for so long, so it's got to go!

If your rabbits are housed in a cage with a wire floor you'll want to put down something solid for the kits to sit on so their feet won't be constantly falling through the wire. My favorite thing is a small square of carpet or plastic "cage liner" (it has holes in it so the poo can fall through), just make sure to keep it clean and dry, carpet may need to be changed regularly.

At this point I also like to give the kits a small dish of food and water that is at their level (which is short), if their mother's food and water containers are higher up than a comfortable level for the kits to reach.

Stone crocks work well for this, as do dishes that can be attached to the side of the cage so that the dish can't be knocked over.

Now all your rabbits (mama and babies) get to go on free-feed, meaning that they always have food in their bowls. This will continue until the kits are old enough to be weaned.

It is also nice to provide the kits will a supply of fresh hay every day. It's not necessary but the rabbits seem to enjoy the treat and it's an easy way to start introducing solid food into a kit's diets. Several breeders say that the extra fiber can help prevent gut-problems with your new kits so it is a good practice to adopt.

Getting Kicked Out of the House - Weaning the Kits

The kits are now seven weeks old. You rabbits are starting to look more like adults then the furry little balls of fluff that they were a few weeks ago. It's time for them to move into their own cage and give mom a break.

You can wean kits as early as five weeks old but I like to wait until seven weeks, when they've really had a chance to grow and taper off the mother's milk supply. You could also wait until eight weeks to wean if you needed, but no longer!

The mama rabbit is usually fed up with her babies by now and you need to separate the littermates before the bucks can start mating and producing more babies. Leaving the kits with the mother too long can also have a negative effect on her health from too much nursing.

Start by removing all the kits into one cage and leaving the mother in her own cage. It nice to leave the kits all together for a few days to a week as it lessens the stress of being removed from their mother, then move everyone into their own cages.

When all the rabbits have their own cages stop with free feeding and go back to a normal feeding schedule using the quantity of food that you usually feed your rabbits.

You can read the bag that your food comes in for

recommended quantities, which will depend on the size of your rabbit. If you'd like more info on feeding you can read a great feeding article by go to our website at www.EverythingRabbit.com and click on the "Rabbit Basics" tab.

At this point you are ready to sell and/or find new homes for the babies (if that's what you want to do) or keep feeding them and let them grow into healthy adult rabbits. **Congratulations, you have just successfully raised your first litter of bunnies!**

Chapter 8

Now What? What to Do After Your First Litter

After your first litter you may be thinking "Woohoo... now what?" In this chapter we'll explore a few ideas that can help you become even more successful as a rabbit breeder and talk about when you can breed your mama rabbit again.

When can I Breed My Doe (female rabbit) Again?

Rabbits can produce a TON of babies in a short period of time, which is probably why they have been a popular source of food for hundreds of years. If you've been bit by the rabbit breeder bug, or are producing rabbits for a hobby farm or homestead, here is the schedule that you can use to re-breed your doe:

If you are on a vigorous breeding schedule you can re-breed your doe when her kits are five weeks old, as long as she is still in good health and hasn't lost any weight. You may have to wait until she is in heat and ready to breed but she can start as early as this.

For a more relaxed schedule, which seems to keep the does in great general health, wait to re-breed her until her kits are eight weeks old. Most does have stopped nursing by then and are ready to have another litter.

Always check to make sure that she is still in good health and hasn't lost any weight, which can happen when a doe has just raised a very large litter. If she looks a little worse for wear then you'll want to give her some time off from babies until she regains the weight she had before she kindled.

How to Keeping Breeding Records

I have a folder on my computer for each doe that I've ever bred. It contains all the information about what buck she was bred to, what day she gave birth, how many kits, was she a good mother, what colors did her kits turn out to be, what problems did I have to solve, etc. This has been a valuable resource over the years and in part, has been a great source of information for writing this book.

If you're a hard-copy kind of person, a three-ring binder and sheet of paper will work just as well for your record keeping. If you're more of a tech person then try using Evernote for your records. It's an online program (and app) that lets you keep all sorts of data organized and close at hand. It will also link across multiple devices so you can look it up from anywhere, anytime.

Keep notes on anything that could be of use later on and any data that you'd been interested in tracking.

How to Make a Pedigree

It's always a great idea to keep a pedigree for all your rabbits, but is almost a requirement if you are breeding show rabbits.

A pedigree is a piece of paper that outlines your rabbit's family tree, starting with the parents and then working backwards to the grandparents and great-grandparents. For show rabbits, if you are planning to register your rabbit with the American Rabbit Breeders Association, you must have a pedigree showing back three generations.

A pedigree can also be a great resource for determining the colors that your kits may be when crossing one rabbit with another. If you know a little bit about rabbit color genetics you can start getting pretty accurate with your predictions.

Identification Tattoo

If you are breeding show rabbits this is also the time to place an identification tattoo in their left ear (so that the judge can tell them apart from all the other show rabbits in their category).

You can do this yourself, if you have rabbit tattoo equipment, or ask a local breeder for help (highly recommended if you've never tattooed a rabbit before). This I.D. tattoo should also be recorded on the rabbit's pedigree.

Showing Rabbits

Participating in rabbit shows can be a great outlet for new rabbit breeders to share their passion and connect with other rabbit owners. If you have kids (or you are under 18) then 4-H or FFA clubs can also be a great source for fun rabbit activities and shows.

If you're interested in showing rabbits and learning more about different rabbit breeds then please visit me at www.EverythingRabbit.com for tons of great information and to connect with others in the rabbit community. The American Rabbit Breeders Association is also a great resource for anyone who wishing to join the world of rabbit shows, you can contact them through their website at www.ARBA.net.

Closing Thoughts

If you ever have any questions I'd be happy to hear from you, please feel free to email me at Sarah@EverythingRabbit.com

While you online please take a moment to visit our website & become part of our rabbit community! (You can see us on the web at www.EverythingRabbit.com) I always look forward to hearing from readers and would love to get stories and photos of your new bunny!

While you're there feel free to check out our amazing newsletter and free downloads that come with this book (like plans to make your own carrying cage, a copy of a rabbit monthly heath checklist and chores checklist).

We'd love to have you sign up & stay connected with us. It's only through your support that we are able to provide all the information on our site for free.

Thank you for purchasing this book! **We'd love it if you would leave a** review on Amazon, **it really does help out!** A portion of our proceeds go towards supporting free rabbit education and 4-H clubs.

We are here to support and encourage every rabbit owner so that you and your bunny can enjoy quality time together.

Once again, thank you for taking the time to read my book and for taking the first steps towards becoming a knowledgeable & experienced rabbit owner. It is my pleasure to be able to provide you with this information, collected from years of hands-on experience and through the advice of countless experts in the rabbit world.

P.S. Keep an eye out for our next book and instructional videos on rabbit handling, behavior and training .

P.P.S. If you're looking for a great guide to rabbit basics and care then check out our book: *The Everything Pet Rabbit Handbook* on Amazon.

Thank you for purchasing our book. Please don't forget to leave a review on Amazon if you have enjoyed this book so that we can make our future revisions even better! It helps us out in so many ways ☺

ATTN. TEACHERS: If you are a kid's club 4-H leader, FFA leader, or home school instructor and would like to receive training material for your group please email me, I'm happy to help!

About the Author

Sarah Martin is the founder of the rabbit authority website www.EverythingRabbit.com and the author of several top books on rabbits and rabbit care.

A Note From Sarah:
My first bunny love started over 20 years ago when a little bundle of fur with big, floppy ears entered my life. I would never be the same again.

I started writing and interviewing top experts from all over the rabbit world (and my own personal experiences as a rabbit breeder/ owner) so that other rabbit lovers, like myself, could have somewhere to gather and find great information on EVERYTHING related to rabbits and bunnies.

All of my books are created as an in-depth guide to help newbie and advanced rabbit people alike expand their knowledge, have fun with their rabbits, and avoid major pitfalls along the way.

This lead me to create www.EverythingRabbit.com , a place to get all your questions answered, to find cool tips and fun activities, and to build a community of people who love rabbits as much as I do.

Wishing you and your furry friends many blessings!

Sarah Martin

By Sarah Martin

21975095R00062

Printed in Great Britain
by Amazon